In Loving Memory Of

____

Forever My Love

"Your memory feels like home to me. So when my mind wanders, it always finds it's way back to you."

The first time we me I felt...

My happiest memory of you is...

My favorite thing that we used to do together is....

When I wake up, my first thoughts are...

The most difficult time of the day is...

"I once had someone who made every day mean something. I miss you, my love."

Something that helps me the most right now is....

Memories of the little things that bring a smile to my heart are...

When I go to our favorite place, I feel...

Your favorite movie was ________________
When I watch it now I feel...

A random memory that keeps coming to mind is...

I was always in awe of the way you...

"Perhaps they are not stars, but openings where our loved ones shine down."

When I really need comfort, I call...

You always made me laugh when...

What I miss the most is...

Some things I do to keep your memory alive are...

Some things that help me through my sadness, are...

Ways that I will be good to myself are...

"To live in the hearts we leave behind is not to die."

Thomas Campbell

The words I need to hear when I am feeling sad, are...

When I was around you, I felt...

The nicest thing that someone said or did for me was...

People around you would always admire ___________

When I think about that now, I feel...

Loving you changed me in these ways...

Your favorite season was ______________

To honor your memory, this year I will...

“The highest tribute to the dead is not grief, but gratitude.”

Thomas Wilder

Something I look forward to, is...

Today I listened to your favorite song.
It made me feel...

Your three best qualities were...

Your unconditional love made me feel...

One thing that would always make you mad was _______________. Thinking of that now makes me feel...

Something that helps me when things are hard, is...

"It's hard to forget someone who gave you so much to remember."

Valuable lessons you taught me about myself are...

One thing I loved doing with you was...

Something that only I knew about you was...

If I could talk to you again,
I would tell you...

A story that epitomizes you perfectly is...

This grief has taught me...

"What we have
once loved we
can never lose;
they become a
part of us."

Our favorite vacation was __________.
My fondest memories of that trip are...

Ways that I will reach out to my support system are...

A time that you surprised me was...

A favorite keepsake that reminds me of you is...

I was so proud of you when...

No matter how bad my day is, when I think of ______________, I feel better

“Graves are the footprints of angels.”

Henry Wadsworth Longfellow

My greatest challenge in life now, is...

The thing that helped the most through my grief is...

Things I wish someone would say to me are...

The kindest thing I can do for myself right now is...

What I hope for myself a year from now is...

Favorite Pictures, Fond Memories

Favorite Pictures, Fond Memories

Favorite Pictures, Fond Memories

Favorite Pictures, Fond Memories

Favorite Pictures, Fond Memories

Favorite Pictures, Fond Memories

Favorite Pictures, Fond Memories

Favorite Pictures, Fond Memories

Favorite Pictures, Fond Memories

Favorite Pictures, Fond Memories

Favorite Pictures, Fond Memories

Favorite Pictures, Fond Memories

Favorite Pictures, Fond Memories

Favorite Pictures, Fond Memories

Made in the USA
Las Vegas, NV
21 October 2021